A Brief History of New York City

KJ Smith

Copyright © 2025 KJ Smith

All rights reserved.

ISBN: 9798316914531

Contents

INTRODUCTION 1

BEFORE THE DUTCH – THE LAND OF LENAPE 3

NEW AMSTERDAM – THE DUTCH COLONY 7

A BRITISH CITY & THE REVOLUTION 11

GROWTH & IMMIGRATION IN THE 19TH CENTURY 15

THE GILDED AGE & THE BIRTH OF THE MODERN CITY 21

THE GREAT DEPRESSION AND THE RISE OF THE MODERN METROPOLIS 27

POST-WAR BOOM & THE CULTURAL REVOLUTION 33

CRISIS, DECLINE & REINVENTION 40

PRESENT NEW YORK 47

CONCLUSION 53

INTRODUCTION

New York City is more than just a place—it's an idea, a symbol of ambition, resilience, and endless possibilities. With its towering skyline, bustling streets, and a cultural influence that spans the globe, it has long been considered the capital of the world. But how did this metropolis, once a small Dutch trading post, grow into one of the most powerful and dynamic cities in history?

This book takes you on a journey through the history of New York, from its earliest days as a Lenape settlement to its rise as a colonial stronghold, its transformation into an industrial powerhouse, and its present-day status as a global leader in finance, culture, and innovation. Along the way, we'll explore the people, events, and movements that shaped the city—waves of immigrants who built its streets, visionaries who redefined its skyline, and moments of triumph and tragedy that tested its resilience.

New York has always been a city of change. Its ability to reinvent itself time and again has made it a unique force in

A BRIEF HISTORY OF NEW YORK

American and world history. From the Revolutionary War to the skyscraper boom, from economic crashes to cultural revolutions, this city has been at the center of it all.

In the following chapters, we will uncover the fascinating stories that made New York what it is today. Whether you are a lifelong New Yorker or someone who dreams of visiting, this book will offer insights into the city's past, helping to understand why New York continues to captivate and inspire people from all walks of life.

Welcome to the story of New York—one that is still being written.

BEFORE THE DUTCH – THE LAND OF LENAPE

Long before the towering skyscrapers and bustling streets of New York City, this land was home to the Lenape people. For thousands of years, the Lenape—part of the larger Algonquian-speaking tribes—inhabited what is now New York, New Jersey, and parts of Pennsylvania and Delaware. They called the area Lenapehoking, meaning "land of the Lenape," and lived in harmony with its forests, rivers, and coastline.

Life Among the Lenape

The Lenape were a semi-nomadic people, moving with the seasons to take advantage of the region's rich natural resources. They lived in small villages of wigwams or longhouses, typically near rivers and estuaries. The Hudson River, which they called Muhheakantuck ("the river that flows both ways"), provided fish, fresh water, and a natural trade route.

They were expert hunters, fishers, and farmers. The "Three

Sisters" of corn, beans, and squash formed the foundation of their agriculture, supplemented by wild game like deer and turkey. The surrounding forests provided nuts, berries, and medicinal plants, which the Lenape used for food and healing.

Trade and Diplomacy

Far from being isolated, the Lenape were active traders and diplomats. They engaged in commerce with other indigenous groups, exchanging furs, shells, and tools. Wampum—small beads made from shells—was particularly valuable, serving both as currency and a means of recording treaties and important agreements.

The Lenape were also known for their peaceful and cooperative nature. Unlike more warlike tribes, they often sought to mediate conflicts rather than engage in long-term warfare. This diplomacy would later shape their interactions with European settlers.

The Arrival of the Europeans

In 1524, the Italian explorer Giovanni da Verrazzano became the first European to sail into New York Harbor. He was followed nearly a century later by Henry Hudson, an Englishman sailing for the Dutch in 1609. Hudson's exploration of the river that now bears his name set the stage for Dutch colonization, and soon, the world of the Lenape would change forever.

At first, trade between the Lenape and the Dutch was mutually beneficial. The Lenape exchanged beaver pelts and other goods for European metal tools, glass beads, and weapons. However, the relationship quickly turned unbalanced. As more settlers arrived, land disputes and conflicts increased. The Dutch, and later the English, viewed land ownership differently than the Lenape, who believed in shared use of the land rather than exclusive possession.

In 1626, the famous (and often misunderstood) purchase of Manhattan took place. According to legend, the Dutch "bought" the island from the Lenape for goods worth around 60 Dutch guilders—often translated to about $24 in modern terms. However, historical evidence suggests that the Lenape may not have understood this as a permanent sale. To them, it was likely seen as an agreement to share the land, not to give it away entirely.

The Displacement of the Lenape

As Dutch and later English settlers expanded their hold on the region, the Lenape were gradually pushed out. Wars, disease, and broken treaties led to the loss of their homeland. Smallpox and other European diseases devastated their population, as they had little immunity to these foreign illnesses. By the late 1700s, most of the surviving Lenape had migrated westward, eventually settling in present-day Oklahoma, Wisconsin, and Canada.

Legacy of the Lenape
Though the Lenape people were displaced, their legacy remains embedded in New York. Many place names—Manhattan, Canarsie, Rockaway—come from their language. Their early trade networks laid the groundwork for New York's rise as a commercial hub. And today, the Lenape continue to preserve their heritage and traditions, keeping their history alive.

A BRIEF HISTORY OF NEW YORK

New York's story begins not with towering buildings or financial empires, but with the people who first called it home. Their connection to the land, their diplomacy, and their resilience set the foundation for the city that would follow.

In the next chapter, we'll explore how a small Dutch trading post called New Amsterdam became the first European foothold in what would one day become one of the greatest cities in the world.

A BRIEF HISTORY OF NEW YORK

NEW AMSTERDAM – THE DUTCH COLONY

When Henry Hudson sailed up the river that would one day bear his name in 1609, he could not have imagined that he was laying the foundation for one of the world's greatest cities. Commissioned by the Dutch East India Company to find a shortcut to Asia, Hudson instead discovered a vast waterway rich in natural resources. His journey sparked Dutch interest in the region, leading to the establishment of a small trading post that would grow into the city of New Amsterdam—New York City's first European settlement.

The Dutch Arrive: A Trading Empire Begins

By the early 1600s, the Dutch had become a dominant force in global trade. The Dutch West India Company, founded in 1621, sought to expand Dutch influence in the Americas. In 1624, the company established the colony of New Netherland, with New Amsterdam as its capital at the southern tip of Manhattan.

A BRIEF HISTORY OF NEW YORK

The primary goal of New Amsterdam was commerce, particularly the lucrative fur trade. The Dutch traded metal tools, beads, and firearms with the indigenous Lenape in exchange for beaver pelts, which were highly valued in Europe. Unlike the Spanish and English, who often sought religious conversion or territorial conquest, the Dutch focused on business.

Life in New Amsterdam

New Amsterdam was a rough but diverse settlement. While its population was small—around 1,500 people by the 1640s—it was remarkably cosmopolitan. Dutch, English, German, Scandinavian, African, and even Jewish settlers lived there, drawn by opportunities for trade and profit.

The town's layout followed the natural contours of the island, with a grid of narrow streets that would later influence modern Manhattan. A wooden wall was built at the northern edge of the settlement to protect against potential attacks from Indigenous groups and English rivals—this later became Wall Street.

Dutch influence extended beyond just trade and urban planning. Many aspects of New York culture can be traced back to these early settlers, including tolerance for religious diversity, a spirit of entrepreneurship, and even place names like Harlem (from Haarlem), Brooklyn (Breukelen), and the Bronx (after Jonas Bronck).

Slavery in New Amsterdam

One often-overlooked part of New Amsterdam's history is its reliance on enslaved labor. The Dutch West India Company brought enslaved Africans to the colony to work on farms, build roads, and construct buildings. However, Dutch slavery differed from the brutal chattel slavery later practiced by the English; some enslaved individuals could earn partial freedoms or own property. Despite this, they remained a vital but exploited part of the colony's workforce.

Peter Stuyvesant and the Expansion of the Colony

In 1647, Peter Stuyvesant became the Director-General of New Netherland. A strict and authoritative leader, Stuyvesant sought to improve the colony's defenses, strengthen its economy, and impose moral order. He built roads, improved sanitation, and established a municipal government. However, he also clashed with settlers who resisted his rigid rule.

One of Stuyvesant's most controversial actions was his opposition to religious freedom. He attempted to ban Jews, Quakers, and Lutherans from practicing their faiths openly, but the Dutch government in Amsterdam overruled him, reinforcing the Netherlands' commitment to religious tolerance. This early precedent for religious freedom would later influence New York's character as a diverse and open society.

The English Takeover (1664)

Despite its prosperity, New Amsterdam remained vulnerable. By the mid-1600s, England was growing more aggressive in expanding its colonial empire. King Charles II sought to claim Dutch territories in North America, granting his brother, the Duke of York, the rights to New Netherland.

A BRIEF HISTORY OF NEW YORK

In 1664, English warships arrived in New Amsterdam's harbor, demanding surrender. Outnumbered and underprepared, Stuyvesant was forced to cede the colony without a fight. The English renamed it New York, in honor of the Duke of York, and the city entered a new era under British rule.

Legacy of New Amsterdam

Though the Dutch rule over New Amsterdam lasted only about 40 years, its impact on New York remains visible today. The city's early commitment to commerce, religious diversity, and cultural openness were all shaped by its Dutch origins. Even common words like "cookie" (from koekje), "boss" (baas), and "stoop" (stoep) come from the Dutch settlers who first walked Manhattan's streets.

The transition from Dutch to English control set the stage for New York's explosive growth in the 18th century. In the next chapter, we'll explore how the city evolved under British rule, its role in the American Revolution, and its transformation from a colonial outpost to a battleground for independence.

A BRITISH CITY & THE REVOLUTION

When the English seized New Amsterdam in 1664, they renamed it New York and ushered in a new era of colonial rule. While many aspects of Dutch life remained—trade, diversity, and religious tolerance—the English brought their own political structures, economic ambitions, and tensions that would eventually lead the city to the forefront of the American Revolution.

New York Under British Rule

Under the English, New York rapidly expanded. The city's strategic location at the mouth of the Hudson River made it a vital hub for commerce and shipping. The population grew as English, Scots, Irish, and French Huguenots joined the mix of Dutch and other European settlers.

The British introduced new governance systems, including English common law, which replaced the Dutch legal system. However, they kept many Dutch traditions, such as religious tolerance and property rights. In contrast to the rigid, Puritan-dominated societies of New England, New York remained a relatively open and multicultural city.

The Growth of Slavery

One of the darker aspects of British rule was the dramatic increase in slavery. By the early 1700s, New York had the largest enslaved population of any northern city. Enslaved Africans worked in homes, on docks, and in businesses, forming a significant part of the city's economy. The fear of rebellion led to harsh restrictions, and in 1712 and 1741, there were uprisings—both of which were brutally suppressed.

Despite these injustices, New York was also home to a growing free Black community that would later play a crucial role in the fight for independence.

New York and the Road to Revolution

By the mid-18th century, tensions between Britain and its American colonies were rising. New York, as a key port and economic center, became a hotbed of political unrest.

- The Stamp Act Crisis (1765): When Britain imposed taxes on printed materials, New Yorkers protested fiercely. A group called the Sons of Liberty formed, organizing demonstrations and boycotts. A British governor's house was burned, and colonial resistance spread.
- Boston Tea Party's Impact (1773): Inspired by Boston's defiance, New Yorkers resisted British taxes on goods, particularly tea. When the British closed Boston's port as

punishment, New York merchants joined the colonial boycott of British goods.

By 1775, war was on the horizon, and New York found itself at the center of the fight for independence.

New York in the American Revolution

When the Revolutionary War began, New York was a key strategic target. Its deep harbor and central location made it essential for both the British and the Continental Army.

- The Battle of Brooklyn (August 1776): This was the first major battle after the Declaration of Independence. General George Washington and his troops fought bravely but were outmaneuvered by the British. In one of the most daring retreats in military history, Washington led his troops across the East River under the cover of fog, narrowly escaping disaster.
- British Occupation (1776–1783): After Washington's retreat, New York became the center of British military operations. For seven years, the city remained under British control, filled with Loyalists (colonists who supported the British) and occupied by enemy troops.
- The Great Fire of 1776: A mysterious fire destroyed a quarter of the city shortly after the British took control. Some believed revolutionaries set it as an act of defiance, though no clear culprit was ever identified.

During the occupation, conditions were brutal. American prisoners of war were held on British prison ships in the harbor, where thousands died from disease and neglect. New York became a city of suffering, caught in the grip of war.

The End of British Rule

In 1783, after the war's final battles and the signing of the Treaty of Paris, the British finally evacuated New York. On November 25, 1783, known as Evacuation Day, Washington's troops marched triumphantly into the city, marking the end of British rule and the beginning of a new era for New York as part of an independent United States.

The Legacy of Revolution

The Revolutionary War left New York forever changed. Once a loyal British colony, it had now played a crucial role in America's fight for independence. Despite years of destruction and hardship, the city would soon rebuild, becoming the financial and political powerhouse of the new nation.

In the next chapter, we'll explore how post-war New York transformed into a booming center of commerce, immigration, and industry, setting the stage for its rise as America's greatest city.

GROWTH & IMMIGRATION IN THE 19TH CENTURY

The end of the American Revolution marked a new beginning for New York City. As the United States emerged as an independent nation, New York became a symbol of the country's potential. Its deep harbor, strategic location, and growing economy made it the country's commercial hub. The city underwent rapid transformation throughout the 19th century, fueled by industrialization, immigration, and the construction of monumental infrastructure. This period laid the foundation for New York to become the metropolis we know today.

The Rise of Commerce and Industry

In the decades following the Revolution, New York's economy boomed. The city capitalized on its prime position on the East Coast and its access to major trade routes, becoming the leading port of entry for goods and people into the United States.

- The Erie Canal (1825): One of the most important events

in New York's growth was the completion of the Erie Canal in 1825. This waterway connected the Hudson River to Lake Erie, opening up vast regions of the Midwest to trade with New York City. The canal made the city an essential point in the transportation of goods like grain, timber, and coal. It also transformed the entire economy of New York State, contributing to the rise of cities like Buffalo and Rochester.
- The Rise of Manufacturing: As the 19th century progressed, New York became a booming industrial city. Factories producing everything from textiles to machinery popped up along the waterfront. The construction of bridges, tunnels, and railroads further cemented the city's role as an industrial and transportation hub.

A City of Immigrants

By the mid-19th century, New York was becoming one of the most diverse cities in the world. Waves of immigrants, driven by famine, poverty, and political unrest in Europe, flooded into the city, transforming its demographics and culture.

- The Irish Famine (1845-1852): The largest group of immigrants during this period came from Ireland. Over a million Irish fled the Great Famine, and many arrived in New York City seeking work and a better life. By the 1850s, the Irish made up a significant portion of the city's population, working mainly as laborers, dock workers, and in the burgeoning construction industry. They also established vibrant neighborhoods, particularly in the Lower East Side and Five Points.
- German Immigrants: The German community also grew

rapidly during the 19th century, escaping political unrest and economic hardship. Many Germans settled in areas like the Bowery and contributed to the city's cultural life through brewing, music, and the arts.
- Italian, Jewish, and Other Immigrants: By the late 19th century, large numbers of Italians and Jews arrived in New York, fleeing poverty, discrimination, and violence in their home countries. They found work in the garment industry, creating a thriving economy around manufacturing. These immigrant groups also shaped the city's cultural identity, contributing to New York's rich tapestry of food, music, and traditions.

New York's reputation as a "melting pot" grew as these various groups brought their languages, traditions, and customs, weaving them into the fabric of the city's diverse society.

The Growth of Urban Infrastructure

As the population of New York exploded, the city faced numerous challenges. The infrastructure could barely keep up with the rapid urbanization, and life in the city was often difficult for its poorest residents.

- Tenement Housing: One of the most significant challenges of the 19th century was the growth of overcrowded tenement housing. Immigrants, often living in squalid conditions, were crammed into small apartments with no ventilation, sanitation, or proper plumbing. The famous Lower East Side tenements, many of which were originally designed for one family, housed dozens of people. These unsanitary conditions led to the spread of disease, and the

city's overcrowded streets were often plagued by poverty and crime.
- The Subway System: New York began addressing its overcrowding issues with the construction of the subway system. In 1904, the first subway line opened, revolutionizing how people moved around the city. The subway became a lifeline for working-class immigrants, connecting neighborhoods that were once isolated and transforming the city into a sprawling urban landscape.

Social and Political Movements

Along with economic growth, the 19th century saw the rise of powerful social and political movements in New York City. These movements sought to address the growing disparities between the rich and poor, advocate for workers' rights, and fight for civil rights.

- Labor Movements: As factories and industries grew, workers began to organize in order to demand better wages, working conditions, and hours. Strikes became common in New York, and the city saw the rise of labor unions, especially among immigrant workers in the garment industry.
- Abolition and Civil Rights: New York was a major center of the abolitionist movement. Many prominent abolitionists, including Frederick Douglass and Sojourner Truth, gave speeches in the city, and New York played an important role in the Underground Railroad, which helped enslaved people escape to freedom. The state of New York officially abolished slavery in 1827, well before the national Emancipation Proclamation.

- Women's Rights: The women's suffrage movement also gained traction in New York, with the famous Seneca Falls Convention held in 1848. Women like Elizabeth Cady Stanton and Susan B. Anthony fought for women's rights, including the right to vote, which would not be realized until 1920.

The Civil War and Its Impact

The outbreak of the Civil War in 1861 had a significant impact on New York City. Although the city was in the Union, it was also home to many Irish immigrants who were sympathetic to the South. This tension reached a breaking point in 1863 with the New York Draft Riots, the largest civil insurrection in the city's history. The riots, sparked by resentment over the draft, led to violent clashes between African Americans, immigrants, and police, resulting in dozens of deaths and widespread destruction.

Despite these divisions, New York ultimately contributed greatly to the Union war effort, supplying soldiers, food, and weapons. After the war, the city's economy boomed, and it became a leader in finance, manufacturing, and trade.

New York's Rise to Dominance

By the end of the 19th century, New York had firmly established itself as the center of American finance and industry. The Stock Exchange, the construction of the Brooklyn Bridge, and the completion of iconic buildings like the Statue of Liberty symbolized the city's unparalleled rise in influence. It became the epicenter of culture, politics, and business in the United States, and the gateway for millions of immigrants seeking a better life.

The foundations laid in this period of growth would shape the city's future, as it expanded and embraced the new century with promise and potential.

In the next chapter, we'll look at the turn of the century, as New York entered a period of remarkable transformation in urban planning, culture, and economic dominance.

A BRIEF HISTORY OF NEW YORK

THE GILDED AGE & THE BIRTH OF THE MODERN CITY

As the 19th century gave way to the 20th, New York City was on the verge of monumental transformation. The turn of the century marked the beginning of the Gilded Age—a period of rapid industrialization, immense wealth accumulation, and stark inequality. It was a time when the city's skyline began to change dramatically, its economy expanded into global markets, and new technologies began to shape every aspect of life. In this chapter, we'll explore how New York became the center of modernity and the birthplace of the city as we know it today.

The Gilded Age: Wealth and Inequality

The late 19th century saw the rise of a new class of industrial magnates and financiers. People like John D. Rockefeller, J.P. Morgan, and Cornelius Vanderbilt amassed vast fortunes and became symbols of the enormous wealth that was being generated by America's rapidly expanding economy. They built railroads, steel mills, and oil empires, and many of them made their homes in New York.

However, the wealth of these so-called "robber barons" was in stark contrast to the poverty and exploitation suffered by the working class. Factory workers, many of whom were immigrants, toiled long hours in dangerous conditions for low wages. The wealth gap between the elite and the poor became increasingly pronounced, leading to the rise of labor movements and social reform efforts. Yet, despite the stark contrast between the rich and the poor, the Gilded Age was also a time of intense innovation and growth that would reshape the city and the country.

The Rise of Skyscrapers and Modern Architecture

One of the most iconic symbols of New York during this period was the skyscraper—the modern building that seemed to reach endlessly into the sky. The late 19th and early 20th centuries saw the birth of the skyscraper as a result of innovations in steel construction and the development of the elevator.

- The Flatiron Building (1902): Completed in 1902, the Flatiron Building was one of the first skyscrapers to truly define the New York skyline. Its distinctive triangular shape was unlike anything else at the time, and it became an instantly recognizable landmark.
- The Woolworth Building (1913): Built by Frank Woolworth, the "five-and-dime" magnate, this 57-story building was one of the tallest in the world when it was completed. Known as the "Cathedral of Commerce," it epitomized the ambition and grandeur of the Gilded Age, symbolizing the city's ascent as a global financial capital.

A BRIEF HISTORY OF NEW YORK

These early skyscrapers changed the city's landscape, making it more vertical and compact. As these monumental buildings began to dominate the skyline, they signaled New York's emergence as the economic powerhouse of the United States.

Immigration and the Transformation of the Lower East Side

The early 20th century saw continued waves of immigration, with millions of people arriving at Ellis Island from Europe. The vast majority of immigrants came seeking work and a better life in the city that promised freedom and opportunity.

- The Lower East Side: This neighborhood became the epicenter of the immigrant experience in New York. Jews, Italians, Poles, and Eastern Europeans poured into the area, many living in overcrowded tenements where they faced poor conditions and limited opportunities. The Lower East Side became a melting pot of cultures, languages, and traditions, and it was here that the cultural fabric of New York truly began to form.
- Jewish Immigrants: Jewish immigrants, fleeing persecution in Eastern Europe and Russia, brought with them a rich cultural heritage. They established vibrant communities, and many would go on to become influential figures in finance, arts, and politics. The Yiddish theater flourished in the Lower East Side, and Jewish immigrants played a major role in the development of the garment industry.

The Subway System: Transforming the City

As New York's population surged, the city's infrastructure

struggled to keep up. The rapid growth of skyscrapers, combined with the influx of immigrants, meant that the city's streets were congested, and transportation became a pressing issue.

In 1904, New York opened its first subway line, revolutionizing how people moved around the city. The subway system was designed to alleviate the congestion on the streets and provide a more efficient way for people to commute. With its low-cost fares and ability to transport thousands of people at once, the subway became the backbone of New York's transportation system and further solidified the city's reputation as the world's most dynamic metropolis.

The creation of the subway also reflected the growing complexity and scale of the city. New York was no longer just a collection of neighborhoods; it was a sprawling urban environment that needed sophisticated systems to support its rapidly expanding population.

The Progressive Era: Reform and Change

While the Gilded Age was a time of immense wealth for some, it was also a time of great social unrest and inequality. The Progressive Era, which began in the late 19th century and continued into the early 20th century, saw a growing movement to address the social, economic, and political problems facing the city.

- Tammany Hall and Political Corruption: In the early 1900s, New York's political system was dominated by Tammany Hall, a powerful political machine. While Tammany provided services and support for immigrants,

it was also notorious for its corruption and exploitation of the poor. Reformers like Theodore Roosevelt and John Purroy Mitchel sought to challenge this system and introduce more transparency and fairness to city politics.
- Social Reform Movements: Progressive reformers fought for better working conditions, child labor laws, and women's suffrage. In 1909, the Triangle Shirtwaist Factory Fire, in which 146 workers, mostly young immigrant women, perished in a preventable disaster, galvanized the city's reform efforts. The tragedy led to widespread calls for labor reform, better working conditions, and the creation of building safety codes.

The Arts and Culture: A New York Renaissance

The early 20th century was also a time of remarkable cultural development. New York City became a hub for the arts, and a new wave of writers, artists, musicians, and performers flocked to the city to make their mark.

- The Harlem Renaissance (1920s): Although the Harlem Renaissance would not reach its height until the 1920s, its roots were planted in the early part of the 20th century. African American artists, writers, and musicians like Langston Hughes, Zora Neale Hurston, and Duke Ellington began to transform the city's cultural landscape, particularly in the Harlem neighborhood, which became the epicenter of African American culture.
- Broadway and the Arts: New York became the heart of American theater, with Broadway leading the way. The city's theaters and music halls attracted the best talent from across the country, and many of the most enduring works

A BRIEF HISTORY OF NEW YORK

of American theater were born in New York during this period.

The Birth of the Modern City

By the time the First World War began in 1914, New York had firmly established itself as the center of American commerce, culture, and politics. The Gilded Age and early 20th century were transformative for the city—this was when New York began to take its modern shape. The construction of skyscrapers, the growth of immigrant communities, the expansion of the subway system, and the rise of social and cultural movements all played a crucial role in shaping the city that would become the greatest metropolis in the world.

In the next chapter, we will explore how New York navigated the challenges of the 20th century—surviving the Great Depression, becoming a symbol of American resilience, and solidifying its position as a global capital in the post-World War II era.

THE GREAT DEPRESSION AND THE RISE OF THE MODERN METROPOLIS

As the 19th century gave way to the 20th, New York City was on the verge of monumental transformation. The turn of the century marked the beginning of the Gilded Age—a period of rapid industrialization, immense wealth accumulation, and stark inequality. It was a time when the city's skyline began to change dramatically, its economy expanded into global markets, and new technologies began to shape every aspect of life. In this chapter, we'll explore how New York became the center of modernity and the birthplace of the city as we know it today.

The Gilded Age: Wealth and Inequality

The late 19th century saw the rise of a new class of industrial magnates and financiers. People like John D. Rockefeller, J.P. Morgan, and Cornelius Vanderbilt amassed vast fortunes and became symbols of the enormous wealth that was being generated by America's rapidly expanding economy. They built railroads, steel mills, and oil empires, and many of them made their homes in New York.

However, the wealth of these so-called "robber barons" was in stark contrast to the poverty and exploitation suffered by the working class. Factory workers, many of whom were immigrants, toiled long hours in dangerous conditions for low wages. The wealth gap between the elite and the poor became increasingly pronounced, leading to the rise of labor movements and social reform efforts. Yet, despite the stark contrast between the rich and the poor, the Gilded Age was also a time of intense innovation and growth that would reshape the city and the country.

The Rise of Skyscrapers and Modern Architecture

One of the most iconic symbols of New York during this period was the skyscraper—the modern building that seemed to reach endlessly into the sky. The late 19th and early 20th centuries saw the birth of the skyscraper as a result of innovations in steel construction and the development of the elevator.

- The Flatiron Building (1902): Completed in 1902, the Flatiron Building was one of the first skyscrapers to truly define the New York skyline. Its distinctive triangular shape was unlike anything else at the time, and it became an instantly recognizable landmark.
- The Woolworth Building (1913): Built by Frank Woolworth, the "five-and-dime" magnate, this 57-story building was one of the tallest in the world when it was completed. Known as the "Cathedral of Commerce," it epitomized the ambition and grandeur of the Gilded Age, symbolizing the city's ascent as a global financial capital.

A BRIEF HISTORY OF NEW YORK

These early skyscrapers changed the city's landscape, making it more vertical and compact. As these monumental buildings began to dominate the skyline, they signaled New York's emergence as the economic powerhouse of the United States.

Immigration and the Transformation of the Lower East Side

The early 20th century saw continued waves of immigration, with millions of people arriving at Ellis Island from Europe. The vast majority of immigrants came seeking work and a better life in the city that promised freedom and opportunity.

- The Lower East Side: This neighborhood became the epicenter of the immigrant experience in New York. Jews, Italians, Poles, and Eastern Europeans poured into the area, many living in overcrowded tenements where they faced poor conditions and limited opportunities. The Lower East Side became a melting pot of cultures, languages, and traditions, and it was here that the cultural fabric of New York truly began to form.
- Jewish Immigrants: Jewish immigrants, fleeing persecution in Eastern Europe and Russia, brought with them a rich cultural heritage. They established vibrant communities, and many would go on to become influential figures in finance, arts, and politics. The Yiddish theater flourished in the Lower East Side, and Jewish immigrants played a major role in the development of the garment industry.

The Subway System: Transforming the City

As New York's population surged, the city's infrastructure

struggled to keep up. The rapid growth of skyscrapers, combined with the influx of immigrants, meant that the city's streets were congested, and transportation became a pressing issue.

In 1904, New York opened its first subway line, revolutionizing how people moved around the city. The subway system was designed to alleviate the congestion on the streets and provide a more efficient way for people to commute. With its low-cost fares and ability to transport thousands of people at once, the subway became the backbone of New York's transportation system and further solidified the city's reputation as the world's most dynamic metropolis.

The creation of the subway also reflected the growing complexity and scale of the city. New York was no longer just a collection of neighborhoods; it was a sprawling urban environment that needed sophisticated systems to support its rapidly expanding population.

The Progressive Era: Reform and Change

While the Gilded Age was a time of immense wealth for some, it was also a time of great social unrest and inequality. The Progressive Era, which began in the late 19th century and continued into the early 20th century, saw a growing movement to address the social, economic, and political problems facing the city.

- Tammany Hall and Political Corruption: In the early 1900s, New York's political system was dominated by Tammany Hall, a powerful political machine. While Tammany provided services and support for immigrants,

it was also notorious for its corruption and exploitation of the poor. Reformers like Theodore Roosevelt and John Purroy Mitchel sought to challenge this system and introduce more transparency and fairness to city politics.
- Social Reform Movements: Progressive reformers fought for better working conditions, child labor laws, and women's suffrage. In 1909, the Triangle Shirtwaist Factory Fire, in which 146 workers, mostly young immigrant women, perished in a preventable disaster, galvanized the city's reform efforts. The tragedy led to widespread calls for labor reform, better working conditions, and the creation of building safety codes.

The Arts and Culture: A New York Renaissance

The early 20th century was also a time of remarkable cultural development. New York City became a hub for the arts, and a new wave of writers, artists, musicians, and performers flocked to the city to make their mark.

- The Harlem Renaissance (1920s): Although the Harlem Renaissance would not reach its height until the 1920s, its roots were planted in the early part of the 20th century. African American artists, writers, and musicians like Langston Hughes, Zora Neale Hurston, and Duke Ellington began to transform the city's cultural landscape, particularly in the Harlem neighborhood, which became the epicenter of African American culture.
- Broadway and the Arts: New York became the heart of American theater, with Broadway leading the way. The city's theaters and music halls attracted the best talent from across the country, and many of the most enduring works

of American theater were born in New York during this period.

The Birth of the Modern City

By the time the First World War began in 1914, New York had firmly established itself as the center of American commerce, culture, and politics. The Gilded Age and early 20th century were transformative for the city—this was when New York began to take its modern shape. The construction of skyscrapers, the growth of immigrant communities, the expansion of the subway system, and the rise of social and cultural movements all played a crucial role in shaping the city that would become the greatest metropolis in the world.

In the next chapter, we will explore how New York navigated the challenges of the 20th century—surviving the Great Depression, becoming a symbol of American resilience, and solidifying its position as a global capital in the post-World War II era.

POST-WAR BOOM & THE CULTURAL REVOLUTION

In the years following World War II, New York City entered a period of unprecedented transformation. Emerging from the devastation of the Great Depression and the global turmoil of the war, the city became a symbol of resilience, prosperity, and opportunity. The post-war era, spanning the 1950s and 1960s, was marked by an economic boom, massive urban development, and profound cultural shifts. In this chapter, we will explore how New York evolved into the global cultural and economic capital it is today, and how the city became a crucible for a cultural revolution that would shape the world.

Economic Prosperity and the Rise of the Middle Class

After World War II, New York's economy experienced an extraordinary period of growth. The war had spurred industrial production, and with the peace came a surge in demand for goods, services, and infrastructure.

A BRIEF HISTORY OF NEW YORK

- The Rise of the Financial District: Wall Street solidified its position as the heart of global finance. With the booming post-war economy, New York became the world's primary financial center. The New York Stock Exchange continued to grow, and international trade flourished, making the city a hub for financial services, banking, and global markets. The rise of multinational corporations also centered their operations in the city, further cementing its economic dominance.

- The Growth of the Middle Class: The prosperity of the post-war years created a flourishing middle class in New York. Families moved into newly constructed suburban homes in places like Long Island and Westchester County, while the city's own residential neighborhoods boomed with apartment complexes and luxury high-rises. The middle class had more disposable income, and New Yorkers enjoyed rising standards of living, with an increase in consumer goods, cars, and household appliances becoming staples of everyday life. The city's new affluence was reflected in the burgeoning retail industries, with flagship department stores like Macy's and Gimbels attracting shoppers from across the globe.

The Growth of the Suburbs and Urban Migration

While New York's economy was thriving, the city was also undergoing significant demographic and spatial changes. The rise of the automobile and the expansion of highways enabled many middle-class families to move out of the city and into the suburbs, setting the stage for a pattern of migration that would continue for decades.

- Suburbanization: The booming automobile industry and the construction of the Interstate Highway System allowed people to live farther from their workplaces. Suburbs like Levittown on Long Island became symbolic of the American dream of homeownership. This migration, however, led to a decline in New York's population as families, seeking larger homes and better schools, left the city in droves.

- Urban Decline and Economic Disparities: As the middle class left for the suburbs, New York's urban core faced significant challenges. The exodus of wealthier residents resulted in the flight of businesses and an erosion of the city's tax base. The city's neighborhoods began to face growing economic inequalities, with many areas falling into disrepair. Public services struggled to meet the needs of a growing population, and social unrest began to simmer beneath the surface.

Cultural Revolution: The Beats, Bohemia, and Counterculture

The 1950s and 1960s were not just decades of economic prosperity—they were also periods of profound social and cultural change. New York, as the cultural epicenter of the world, played a central role in the development of movements that would challenge traditional norms and reshape society.

- The Beat Generation and the Rise of Bohemia: In the 1950s, New York was home to the nascent Beat Generation, a group of writers and artists who rejected conventional social structures and sought new forms of self-expression. Writers like Jack Kerouac, Allen Ginsberg, and William S. Burroughs became icons of the counterculture, using their work to explore themes of personal freedom, spirituality, and rebellion against societal expectations. The Beats found their base in neighborhoods like Greenwich Village, which became the epicenter of bohemian life in the city.

- The 1960s: A New Era of Revolution: The cultural upheaval of the 1960s, fueled by the civil rights movement, anti-war protests, and the rise of feminism, reached a fever pitch in New York. The city was a hotbed for political activism, with Columbia University at the center of student protests against the Vietnam War. At the same time, the city was experiencing a sexual revolution, epitomized by the opening of the first gay bars and the burgeoning LGBTQ+ rights movement. The 1969 Stonewall Riots in the Greenwich Village area were a watershed moment in the fight for LGBTQ+ rights, marking the beginning of the modern LGBTQ+ rights movement.

The Birth of Modern Art: Abstract Expressionism and Pop Art

The post-war years also saw New York solidify its position as the world's leading center of contemporary art. The city's galleries, museums, and cultural institutions became incubators for new artistic movements that would revolutionize the art world.

- Abstract Expressionism: In the 1940s and 1950s, New York became the epicenter of Abstract Expressionism, a movement that rejected traditional forms and embraced spontaneous, expressive techniques. Artists like Jackson Pollock, Willem de Kooning, and Mark Rothko created large-scale, emotionally charged works that challenged viewers to rethink their perceptions of art. New York's Museum of Modern Art (MoMA) and the Metropolitan Museum of Art became influential players in promoting these new styles, cementing the city's status as the global capital of contemporary art.

- Pop Art: The 1960s saw the rise of Pop Art, which embraced mass media, advertising, and consumer culture. Led by artists like Andy Warhol, Roy Lichtenstein, and Claes Oldenburg, Pop Art blurred the line between high culture and popular culture, turning everyday objects and celebrities into art. Warhol's famous Campbell's Soup Cans and Marilyn Monroe portraits became symbols of the era's obsession with consumerism, fame, and mass production. New York's SoHo district became the hub of the Pop Art movement, with artists flocking to its lofts and galleries.

The Rise of the Nightlife Scene and Music Revolution

In addition to the visual arts, the 1950s and 1960s saw a vibrant transformation in New York's music and nightlife scenes. The city's streets were alive with jazz, rock, and soul, giving rise to a cultural revolution in both music and entertainment.

- Jazz in New York: The city had long been a center for jazz, but in the post-war years, it became the undisputed capital of the genre. Clubs in Harlem and Greenwich Village, like the Village Vanguard and the Apollo Theater, hosted legendary performances by figures like Charlie Parker, Dizzy Gillespie, and Thelonious Monk. The sound of jazz echoed through New York's nightclubs and contributed to the city's reputation as a global center of musical innovation.

- Rock and Roll: As the 1960s wore on, the sound of rock and roll took over New York's music scene. The Stonewall Inn became a center of LGBTQ+ culture, and venues like the Fillmore East hosted some of the most famous rock concerts of the era, with bands like The Velvet Underground and The Doors performing to sold-out crowds. New York's vibrant music scene played a key role in the cultural revolution of the 1960s, pushing boundaries and challenging the status quo.

The Civil Rights Movement and New York's Social Change

The 1960s was also a time when New York was at the forefront of the civil rights movement. The city became a center for political activism, with major protests and marches calling for racial equality, fair housing, and social justice.

- The Civil Rights Movement: New York played a significant role in the national struggle for civil rights. Prominent activists like Malcolm X and Rosa Parks spent time in the city, and the March on Washington in 1963, where Dr. Martin Luther King Jr. delivered his famous "I Have a Dream" speech, was widely supported by New Yorkers. The city's African American community, particularly in Harlem, was a key player in pushing for desegregation and voting rights for Black Americans.

- The 1964 Civil Rights Act and Fair Housing Act: These landmark pieces of legislation, passed during the 1960s, aimed to eliminate segregation in public places and promote equal housing opportunities. They represented the culmination of years of activism and were significant victories for civil rights leaders in New York and across the nation.

Conclusion: The Shaping of Modern New York

The 1950s and 1960s were decades of immense change for New York City. As the city recovered from the trials of the Depression and the war, it became a global center of culture, finance, and political activism. The post-war economic boom, combined with social movements, cultural revolutions, and the growth of new artistic movements, transformed the city into a vibrant and diverse metropolis.

By the 1970s, New York had firmly established its place as a hub of global culture, and its role as a cultural and economic powerhouse would only continue to grow in the decades to come. In the next chapter, we'll examine how New York faced the challenges of the 1970s—rising crime, fiscal crises, and urban decay—while continuing to redefine itself as the city of reinvention and resilience.

CRISIS, DECLINE & REINVENTION

The 1970s and 1980s were a period of immense struggle for New York City, yet they were also times of profound reinvention. The city grappled with mounting fiscal crises, rising crime rates, urban decay, and a shrinking industrial base. However, in the face of adversity, New York would once again demonstrate its resilience and capacity for transformation. In this chapter, we will explore the crises that nearly led to the city's collapse and the extraordinary efforts made to revive it.

The Fiscal Crisis of the 1970s: Bankruptcy and Recovery

The 1970s began with a sense of unease. While New York was still reeling from the changes of the 1960s, the city soon faced a fiscal crisis that threatened to derail its progress and destabilize its economy.

- The City's Economic Woes: By the early 1970s, New York was in deep financial trouble. The city's once-thriving manufacturing base was in decline, while welfare and social service costs were soaring. City government overspending and reliance on borrowed money led to a massive budget deficit, and by 1975, New York City was on the brink of bankruptcy. The New York Times famously headline read, "Ford to City: Drop Dead," referring to President Gerald Ford's refusal to offer federal bailouts.

- The Bankruptcy and the Emergency Control Board: The city did not declare bankruptcy, but its finances were under such strain that it had to be taken over by the Emergency Financial Control Board, a body created to oversee New York's budget and impose austerity measures. Mayor Abraham Beame, who had assumed office in 1974, was forced to slash budgets, raise taxes, and negotiate tough labor contracts. As a result, public services were cut, including police and fire departments, and unemployment rose.

- Austerity and Discontent: The fiscal crisis left many New Yorkers frustrated. The city became an unsafe and dirty place. Many neighborhoods fell into disrepair, with a noticeable increase in poverty and a decline in quality of life. Crime rates skyrocketed, and iconic landmarks like Grand Central Terminal were left in a state of neglect. As New York City seemed to teeter on the brink of collapse, it appeared as if the city that had once been an engine of progress was failing.

The Rise in Crime and the Struggle for Safety

As the fiscal crisis intensified, New York City's crime rate surged, further contributing to the city's sense of decay. The

A BRIEF HISTORY OF NEW YORK

1970s and 1980s were marked by a pervasive sense of danger, as crime spiked across the boroughs.

- The "Bad Old Days" of Crime: New York became synonymous with crime during this era. Street gangs, drugs, and violent crimes were rampant in neighborhoods like Times Square, Harlem, and South Bronx. The Son of Sam killings in 1976-1977, the rise of crack cocaine in the 1980s, and the notorious "crack epidemic" made the city feel out of control. In 1979, there were 2,245 homicides in New York, a number that remains shockingly high even today. Public transportation was unsafe, and many areas were considered off-limits after dark.

- The Fear Factor: Fear gripped many residents, with New Yorkers growing wary of walking the streets, especially in poorer neighborhoods. The city's once-vibrant nightlife, including its theater and music scenes, began to wither as people stayed home for safety reasons. Tourism also took a hit, and businesses were hesitant to invest in a city seen as dangerous.

The Decline of New York's Industrial Base and Urban Decay

In the 1970s and 1980s, New York faced an industrial exodus as factories and manufacturing jobs left the city, seeking cheaper labor elsewhere in the U.S. or overseas. The city's economy, once reliant on heavy industry, struggled to adapt to the changing times.

- Deindustrialization and Job Losses: New York had once been a manufacturing powerhouse, with jobs in industries such as textiles, furniture-making, and shipbuilding. However, as globalization took hold, many factories closed or relocated to more cost-effective locations. This deindustrialization led to massive job losses, particularly in working-class neighborhoods like Brooklyn, Queens, and the Bronx. At the same time, the service sector failed to create enough new jobs to replace those lost in manufacturing.

- Urban Decay and the Decline of Housing: As the economy struggled, many neighborhoods fell into disrepair. The Bronx, in particular, became infamous for arson and abandoned buildings. Over 40,000 buildings were torched in the Bronx during the 1970s, contributing to the perception of the city as a dangerous, decaying place. Housing projects built in the mid-20th century became overcrowded and rife with poverty, and entire city blocks became abandoned, with people fleeing to the suburbs or elsewhere in search of safety and security.

- Times Square and the "Gritty" Image: Times Square, once a bright and bustling entertainment district, became a symbol of New York's decline. The area became known for its adult entertainment, crime, and decay. The neon lights of Broadway theaters faded, and the streets were littered with drugs, prostitution, and crime. By the end of the 1970s, Times Square was a shadow of its former self.

Reinvention: The Efforts to Revive New York City

Despite the grim picture painted by the 1970s and early 1980s, New York City did not stay in decline for long. By the mid-1980s,

A BRIEF HISTORY OF NEW YORK

a series of reforms, investments, and leadership changes began to turn the city around. A new vision for New York emerged, one focused on revitalization and reinvention.

- The Election of Mayor Ed Koch (1978–1989): In 1977, New York elected Ed Koch as mayor. His leadership marked the beginning of a long period of reinvention for the city. He took steps to restore fiscal stability by aggressively negotiating with unions and securing federal and state aid. His administration cleaned up the streets, reintroduced law and order, and began the slow process of rebuilding the city's infrastructure. Koch's tenure also included efforts to revitalize neighborhoods and improve public services.

- The Clean-Up and Rebuilding of Times Square: One of Koch's lasting legacies was his role in the transformation of Times Square. Under his leadership, the city began to clean up the district and attract more mainstream entertainment businesses. A large-scale redevelopment plan started to bring in corporate investment, and by the 1990s, the area began to regain its status as an entertainment hub, albeit in a very different form from its past.

- The Decline of Crime: The Birth of "Safe Streets": In the late 1980s, the city began to crack down on crime. With the appointment of William Bratton as police commissioner in 1994, the city introduced new strategies such as "broken windows policing", which focused on cracking down on minor offenses like fare evasion, graffiti, and disorderly conduct. By the end of the 1980s and early

1990s, crime rates in the city began to fall dramatically, restoring a sense of safety.

- The Arrival of Wall Street and the Financial Rebirth: The late 1980s also saw a resurgence in New York's financial industry, which helped to bring the city back to prosperity. The booming financial markets led to a massive growth in real estate development. Skyscrapers rose once again, and the city's financial center regained its dominance on the global stage. The combination of public safety initiatives, fiscal discipline, and private investment helped New York begin its reinvention into the prosperous metropolis that would characterize the 1990s.

Cultural Renaissance and the Revival of the Arts

While the economic and political efforts to revitalize New York were ongoing, the cultural scene was also undergoing a significant transformation. By the 1980s, artists, musicians, and performers were returning to the city's neighborhoods, bringing with them a new wave of creativity.

- The Downtown Arts Scene: SoHo, Chelsea, and Greenwich Village became hotbeds of artistic activity once more, with galleries and artists' lofts proliferating in the 1980s. The avant-garde art world, along with experimental theater and music, came back to life, and New York remained a magnet for creative individuals.

- Hip-Hop and the Rise of Street Culture: The 1980s also witnessed the emergence of hip-hop culture, which would become a defining force in global music and fashion. New

York's South Bronx was the birthplace of hip-hop, with pioneers like DJ Kool Herc, Grandmaster Flash, and Run-D.M.C. influencing a cultural revolution in music, dance, fashion, and language.

Conclusion: From Crisis to Renaissance

The 1970s and 1980s were marked by some of the most challenging years in New York's history. The fiscal crisis, rising crime, urban decay, and the collapse of traditional industries threatened the city's future. However, by the end of the 1980s, New York had begun to rebound. Through smart leadership, investment, and a cultural resurgence, New York reinvented itself as a place of both economic prosperity and artistic innovation.

As we move into the 1990s, the city's future looked brighter than ever. In the next chapter, we'll explore how New York reached new heights of global influence in the 1990s and beyond, embracing its role as a diverse, cosmopolitan, and world-renowned city.

PRESENT NEW YORK

The final decades of the 20th century and the dawn of the 21st century marked a period of remarkable transformation for New York City. Having emerged from the fiscal and social crises of the 1970s and 1980s, the city was now poised to step into the global spotlight, asserting itself as not only the financial capital of the world but also a cultural and technological powerhouse. This chapter examines the resurgence of New York City during the 1990s and into the 21st century, exploring how it reinvented itself as a thriving, diverse metropolis that continues to shape global trends in business, culture, and society.

The 1990s: Economic Resurgence and the Rise of Globalization

The 1990s were defined by the city's economic recovery and the rapid globalization that reshaped both its economy and identity. Under the leadership of Mayor Rudy Giuliani (1994–2001), New York City embraced bold initiatives to reclaim its status as the world's most important financial, cultural, and commercial hub.

- Financial Boom and Wall Street's Dominance: In the 1990s, New York's financial sector was booming. The New York Stock Exchange (NYSE) and the NASDAQ grew significantly, fueled by the dot-com revolution and booming stock markets. The city's role as the center of global finance was solidified, as international companies flocked to set up their headquarters in the city, while investment banks, hedge funds, and private equity firms thrived.

- The Tech and Media Revolutions: While the city's financial prowess remained strong, a second wave of transformation came with the rise of technology and media. In the early 1990s, Silicon Alley, the New York counterpart to Silicon Valley, emerged as a hub for technology startups. Companies like AOL, Yahoo!, and Google established significant presences in the city, and the advent of the internet changed the way business was done. Meanwhile, New York remained the epicenter of media with publishing giants like Time Warner, Condé Nast, and NBC shaping global news and entertainment.

- Gentrification and Urban Revival: The economic boom led to gentrification in many neighborhoods that had once been devastated by crime and economic decline. Areas such as SoHo, Greenwich Village, and Williamsburg in Brooklyn became prime real estate for young professionals and artists, leading to the transformation of once-neglected neighborhoods into vibrant centers of creativity, commerce, and luxury living. This process, however, also led to displacement and rising costs for longtime residents, contributing to debates over the future of New York's diverse communities.

A BRIEF HISTORY OF NEW YORK

Cultural Renaissance: Art, Music, and Broadway

The 1990s also saw a resurgence in New York's cultural scene, which had begun to recover in the 1980s but truly flourished in the following decade. The city once again became the global capital of artistic innovation, attracting talent from all over the world.

- The Broadway Boom: One of the most significant cultural developments of the 1990s was the revitalization of Broadway. With the rise of megahit shows like The Lion King, Rent, and Chicago, Broadway once again became a major driver of tourism and the entertainment industry in the city. Theaters, restaurants, and hotels in Times Square boomed, and the district regained its former glory as a symbol of New York's cultural vitality.

- The Art Scene Flourishes: The art scene in New York also flourished in the 1990s. Downtown galleries and museums, such as The Museum of Modern Art (MoMA), The Whitney Museum of American Art, and the Guggenheim Museum, featured provocative and boundary-pushing works. The city also saw an influx of international artists, making it a center of global artistic exchange. During this time, the East Village and Chelsea emerged as epicenters for contemporary art, while the Brooklyn Museum and The Brooklyn Academy of Music (BAM) became key cultural institutions.

- Hip-Hop and the Music Scene: In the 1990s, New York continued to lead the global music scene, particularly through the rise of hip-hop. With artists like Notorious B.I.G., Jay-Z, and Nas, New York solidified its role as the birthplace of hip-hop and rap. The Bronx continued to be the home of many influential hip-hop figures, while Manhattan and Brooklyn saw an explosion of rap battles, club nights, and studio collaborations. This period also saw the rise of R&B and Latin music, with venues like The Apollo Theater and Roseland Ballroom hosting iconic performances.

New York in the Shadow of 9/11

The September 11, 2001 attacks were a defining moment for New York and for the United States. The destruction of the World Trade Center and the devastating loss of life represented one of the darkest days in the city's history. In this chapter, we explore how New York faced the aftermath of the attacks and emerged stronger and more unified than ever.

- The Immediate Aftermath: The attacks on the World Trade Center left New York in shock and mourning. The city, and the world, watched in horror as the Twin Towers collapsed, and over 3,000 lives were lost. In the days following, New York became a symbol of resilience as thousands of first responders, volunteers, and city workers rushed to aid recovery efforts at Ground Zero.

- Rebuilding and Resilience: In the years after 9/11, New York's determination to rebuild was evident. The Freedom Tower, later known as One World Trade Center, became a symbol of New York's strength and resolve. The city rallied together, and the skyline was transformed once again. The 9/11 Memorial and Museum, located at the World Trade Center site, became a poignant reminder of the lives lost and the resilience of the city.

- Security and Surveillance: The attacks also led to a dramatic increase in security measures throughout the city, with the creation of the New York City Police Department's (NYPD) Counterterrorism Bureau and increased surveillance in public spaces. While these measures helped to protect the city, they also raised questions about privacy and civil liberties.

New York's Role in the 21st Century: A Global Metropolis

As the city entered the 21st century, New York continued to evolve into a dynamic and diverse global metropolis.

- Immigration and Diversity: New York has always been a city of immigrants, and in the 21st century, this diversity became even more pronounced. Immigrants from countries all over the world continue to make New York their home, contributing to the city's vibrant culture. Neighborhoods like Chinatown, Little Italy, Jackson Heights, and Flushing in Queens have grown increasingly diverse, showcasing the cultural richness that defines the city. The city remains a beacon for people seeking better opportunities, particularly from countries in Africa, Asia, and Latin America.

- Technology and Innovation: New York's tech industry continued to grow throughout the 21st century, cementing the city's reputation as a hub for innovation. The tech community flourished in Silicon Alley, and companies like Google, Facebook, and Amazon expanded their presence in the city. The rise of fintech and e-commerce companies in the city demonstrated New York's ability to adapt to new industries and technologies, positioning it as a global leader in both finance and innovation.

A BRIEF HISTORY OF NEW YORK

- Cultural Diversity and the Arts: New York's arts scene continued to thrive, with new cultural hubs emerging throughout the city. Institutions like the Brooklyn Academy of Music (BAM) and The Shed in Hudson Yards pushed the boundaries of the arts, while the explosion of festivals like New York Fashion Week, the Tribeca Film Festival, and Harlem Week highlighted the city's global cultural influence. The Museum of Modern Art and the Metropolitan Museum of Art remain iconic institutions, while new spaces like The Vessel at Hudson Yards symbolize New York's continued emphasis on innovation in both the arts and architecture.

New York's journey from the brink of bankruptcy and decline to global prominence and resilience in the face of adversity is nothing short of remarkable. Throughout its history, New York has been a city of reinvention. Whether recovering from the Great Depression, leading the cultural revolutions of the 1960s, or rebounding from the tragedy of 9/11, New York has consistently proven its ability to reinvent itself and to emerge stronger, more diverse, and more dynamic than before.

Today, New York City stands as one of the most influential cities in the world—a hub for finance, culture, art, fashion, technology, and social innovation. It is a testament to the power of resilience, diversity, and the unyielding spirit of its people. New York remains a beacon for dreamers, innovators, and those who believe that anything is possible.

CONCLUSION

New York City, a place of extraordinary contradictions, has long captured the imagination of the world. It is a city that never sleeps, a city that constantly evolves, and a city that never ceases to inspire. From its humble beginnings as a Dutch trading post on the tip of Manhattan Island to its current standing as one of the most influential global metropolises, New York has always been a city on the move—driven by ambition, dreams, and an unshakable resilience.

This book has traced the journey of New York City through its many phases of growth and transformation: from the early colonial period, through the rise of industry, the social upheavals of the 20th century, to the present day, where it stands at the intersection of technology, culture, finance, and social change. Each chapter has highlighted how New York's ability to adapt to changing circumstances has shaped not only the city itself but the wider world.

A City of Reinvention and Resilience

A BRIEF HISTORY OF NEW YORK

New York has always been a city defined by its ability to reinvent itself. In the 19th century, it was the center of American industrialization and immigration. By the 20th century, it had solidified its status as a financial powerhouse and cultural epicenter. Even when faced with adversity—be it the fiscal crises of the 1970s, the devastation of September 11, or the challenges of the COVID-19 pandemic—New York has always emerged stronger, more united, and more determined to thrive.

This resilience is deeply embedded in the DNA of New Yorkers. The city's people are its heartbeat—diverse, driven, and undeterred by obstacles. Whether rebuilding after a disaster or embracing new technologies, New Yorkers have an uncanny ability to turn challenges into opportunities, to find new ways to grow and succeed, even in the face of hardship.

The Power of Diversity

One of the defining features of New York City is its diversity. Over the centuries, immigrants from all corners of the world have made the city their home, and this rich cultural mosaic has become one of its greatest strengths. From the streets of Chinatown to the neighborhoods of Brooklyn, from the vibrant Latino communities of Queens to the artistic enclaves of the East Village, New York is a microcosm of the global community.

This diversity has fueled the city's creativity, its economic vitality, and its global influence. The convergence of different cultures has led to innovations in art, music, food, and fashion. The city's melting pot of ideas, perspectives, and talents has made it a hub for cultural exchange and a source of inspiration for generations of thinkers, artists, and entrepreneurs.

In an age of increasing globalization and migration, New York's role as a city of immigrants and as a beacon for opportunity will continue to shape its future. The ongoing influx of people from around the world will keep the city dynamic and ever-evolving, ensuring that its cultural vibrancy and economic resilience endure.

Challenges and Opportunities Ahead

As we look toward the future, New York faces several challenges. Climate change, the rise of new technologies, the issue of affordable housing, and the changing dynamics of work and education all pose significant hurdles. However, New York has always been a city that embraces change. With its robust infrastructure, its innovative spirit, and its long history of overcoming adversity, the city is well-positioned to meet these challenges head-on.

The continued development of sustainable infrastructure, the advancement of smart technologies, and the commitment to social equity will play pivotal roles in shaping New York's future. The city's ability to adapt to the digital age, while remaining true to its core values of diversity, opportunity, and resilience, will ensure its continued prominence on the global stage.

Moreover, New York's role as a cultural, financial, and technological hub will only continue to grow. From the rise of Silicon Alley to the reinvention of its waterfronts, New York is poised to remain a leader in innovation and creativity. The city's artistic and cultural sectors will continue to evolve, driven by new technologies and global trends, while the city's economy will continue to adapt to the new realities of a digital and interconnected world.

A Legacy of Innovation and Inspiration

In the end, New York's legacy is one of constant reinvention and boundless ambition. It is a city that has consistently defied the odds, reinvented itself when necessary, and inspired the world. From its towering skyscrapers to its intimate neighborhoods, from its bustling streets to its quiet parks, New York embodies the possibilities that exist when creativity, hard work, and diversity come together.

The future of New York City is, like its past, full of possibility. It will continue to be a place where dreams are made, where cultures intersect, and where people from all walks of life come together to create something greater than the sum of its parts. It will remain a city of challenges, yes, but also a city of infinite potential—a city where the impossible becomes possible and where the world comes to dream, work, and live.

As the city moves into its next chapter, one thing is certain: New York will continue to be a symbol of resilience, creativity, and progress. It is a city that never stops moving, a city that always looks forward, and a city that will continue to shape the world for generations to come.

In the words of the famous lyricist George Gershwin in his iconic song "New York, New York," it's the place where "the lights are bright, the city's so nice." New York City, with its enduring energy, innovation, and diversity, will remain an unparalleled beacon of possibility—a city that, despite all its challenges, will never stop striving for greatness.

Final Thought: The Heart of New York

New York City may be a place of constant change, but its heart remains the same. It is a place where people from all walks of life come together to pursue their dreams, where ideas are born, and where the impossible is achieved. It is a place where anything is possible, where every corner of the city has its own story to tell, and where the spirit of resilience continues to drive it forward.

As we close this book, we remember that New York's story is far from over. The city that has witnessed so much—the triumphs and tragedies, the successes and failures—will continue to write its own future. And in that future, one thing is certain: New York City will remain a symbol of endless opportunity, an enduring testament to the power of reinvention, and a city that will continue to capture the world's imagination for years to come.

The story of New York City, in all its glory and complexity, will always be a story worth telling. And it is a story that, for many, will never truly end.

A BRIEF HISTORY OF NEW YORK

Printed in Dunstable, United Kingdom